ACHIEVE LEVEL 5

MATHEMATICS

By **Richard Cooper** and **Shirley Armer**

RISING ★ STARS

Rising Stars UK Ltd, 76 Farnaby Road, Bromley, BR1 4BH
Website: www.risingstars-uk.com

Every effort has been made to trace copyright holders and obtain their
permission for the use of copyright material. The authors and publishers will
gladly receive information enabling them to rectify any error or omission in
subsequent editions.

All facts are correct at time of going to press.

Published 2002
New Edition
Text, design and layout © Rising Stars UK Ltd.

Editorial: Tanya Solomons
Design: Marc Burville-Riley, Claire Harvey
Illustration: copyright © Marc Burville-Riley
Cover photo: copyright © GETTY IMAGES/Olivier Ribardiere

British Library Cataloguing in Publication Data
A CIP record for this book is available from the British Library.

ISBN: 0-9542202-1-8

Printed in Grimsby, UK.

Contents

How to use this book

1 **Introduction Section** – This section tells you what you need to do to get a Level 5. It picks out the key learning objective and explains it simply to you.

2 **The Question** – The question helps you to learn by doing. It is presented in a similar way to a SATs question and gives you a real example to work with.

3 **The Flow Chart** – This shows you the steps to use when completing questions like this. Some of the advice appears on every flow chart (read the question then read it again). This is because this is the best way of getting good marks on the test.

4 **The Tip Boxes** – These provide test hints and general tips on getting the best marks in the SATs.

What we have included:

★ Those topics at Level 4 that are trickiest to get right.

★ ALL Level 5 content so you know that you are covering all the topics that could come up in the test.

Decimals

To achieve Level 5 you must be able to [...] with numbers to two decimal places. Decimals are easy – remember, money is written [...] cimals! For example, £9.85 is nearly £10.00; 3.07 is a bit more than 3.

Let's try some questions.

Question: Write [...] e missing number.

$3.51 \times 4.9 =$ ☐

1 Read the question then read it again.

$3.51 \times 4.9 = ?$ 👁

2 Picture the numbers. What do they look like?

3.51 is around halfway between 3 and 4. 4.9 is just less than 5.

3 Study the numbers again and think about them!

You know the answer is going to be more than 12 (3 x 4) and less than 20 (4 x 5). Remember there is a total of **three** numbers to the right of the decimal points.

4 When multiplying and dividing rem[...] decimal point and calculate.

$$\begin{array}{r} 351 \\ \times\ 49 \\ \hline 3159 \\ 14040 \\ \hline 17199 \end{array}$$

✏

5 Check back to your estimate at Step 3.

You know that your number is going to be between 12 and 20 (see Step 3).

6 Replace the decimal point.

Count **three** in from the right (see Step 3). Your answer is 17.199!

7 Round up or down so you only have 2 numbers after the decimal point.

17.199 becomes 17.20 when you round to two decimal places.

8 If your answer looks sensible, write it in the box.

If it doesn't look right, go back to Step 3 and try again.

Tip 1
When rounding, remember 5 is a[...]P!

$1.265 = 1.27$

Tip 2
When writing money remember:
£0.45p (X)   £0.45 (✓)
0.45p (X)   45p (✓)
Say the answer to yourself before you write it down!

Here is another 'decimals' question we can try together. There are some questions at the bottom of the page for you to try on your own!

Question: $(6.73 - [...]89) + 1.25 =$ ☐

1 Read the question then read it again.

$(6.73 - 4.89) + 1.25 = ?$ 👁

2 Picture the numbers. What do they look like?

6.73 is getting close to 7.
4.89 is nearly 5.
1.25 is a bit more than 1.

3 Study the numbers again and think about them!

$7 - 5 = 2$
2 + 1 and a bit = 3 and a bit

4 Calculate.

Remember – always do the bits in brackets first!

$$\begin{array}{cc} i)\quad 6.73 & ii)\quad 1.84 \\ -\ 4.89 & +\ 1.25 \\ \hline 1.84 & 3.09 \end{array}$$

✏

5 Check back to your estimate at Step 3.

You know that your number is going to be a bit more than 3 (see Step 3 above).

6 Make sure your decimal point is in the right place.

Your answer is 3.09!

7 Round up or down so you only have two numbers after the decimal point.

You only have two numbers after the decimal point so you don't need to do anything!

8 If your answer looks sensible, write it in the box.

If it doesn't – go back to Step 3 and try again.

Practice Questions

Here are some quest[...] you to try [...] Remember to use th[...] step approach above.

1   $(2.3 + 4.75) \times 5.91 =$ ☐

2   $£20 - (£4.62 \times 3) =$ ☐

5 **The Second Question –** On most pages there will be a second question. This will either look at a slightly different question type or give you another example to work through.

6 **The Practice Questions –** This is where you have to do the work! Try the question using the technique in the flow chart then check your answers at the back. Practising questions is the best way to help improve your understanding.

★ We have also put in a big selection of our favourite test techniques, tips for revision and some advice on what the tests are all about, as well as the answers so you can see how well you are getting on.

GOOD LUCK!

Predicting Sequences

This is not as difficult as it sounds. Sequences and patterns just can't live without each other!

Just remember: sequence = numbers following a pattern.

Pattern 1

The pattern may mean the difference between the numbers is always the same:

2   4   6   8   10

+2   +2   +2   +2

Pattern 2

The pattern may mean that the difference between the numbers changes according to a rule:

5   11   23   41   65

+6   +12   +18   +24   (6 times table)

Let's try a typical question.

Question: Predict the next numbers in this sequence:

3, 14, 25, 36, __, __

1 Read the question then read it again.   What is the pattern?

2 Study the numbers.   What is the difference between the numbers?

$3 + ? = 14$ $? = 11$

$14 + ? + 25$ $? = 11$

3 Test the pattern.   Is the difference between all numbers 11?

3   14   25   36   **47**   **58**

+11   +11   +11   +11   +11

4 Does the sequence work? If so, write in the next two numbers.   Yes, the pattern works and the next numbers in the sequence are **47** and **58**.

Tip 1

You will see the pattern more easily if you write in the numbers underneath the sequence.

4   **14**   **34**   **64**

+10   +20   +30

Tip 2

A sequence may be shown in pictures. Just turn the pictures into numbers to help you see the pattern.

✱   ✱✱   ✱✱   ✱✱✱✱
                ✱✱   ✱✱✱

Can be written as

1   2   4   7

+1   +2   +3

Calculators

Calculators can be seen as the answer to everything in Maths. If used correctly they are a useful tool but when used incorrectly they can become a nightmare!

There are a number of steps you can follow to succeed with calculators.

1 Read the question then read it again.

Does the question need a calculator?
Can you work out the question in your head?

2 Press the keys carefully and methodically.

Think clearly. Talk through the calculation in your mind.

3 Check the calculator display.

Always check to see if you have pressed the right buttons.

4 Make sure you press the equals key (=) after each calculation.

Do not forget to do this!

5 Does your final answer look sensible? If not, go back to Step 1.

If you feel the need to redo a calculation, don't hold back. A couple of seconds redoing a sum could save you a couple of marks!

Practice Questions
Try these sums on your calculator.

1   951 + 357 =

3   963 ÷ 12 =

2   101 – 1.1 =

4   87 x 6.7 =

Tip
Don't forget to press the decimal point key when keying in decimal numbers.

3.5 = **3** **.** **5**

2D Shapes

It is important to learn all the precise terms for shapes and their properties. In previous tests the following shapes caught lots of pupils out!

Pentagon

Pentagons have FIVE sides.

Regular pentagons have FIVE EQUAL SIDES.

Remember that a pentagon can become a person!

Parallelogram

A parallelogram is a RECTANGLE THAT HAS BEEN PUSHED OVER.

Remember the opposite sides are the same length but parallel.

Isosceles and Scalene Triangles

An isosceles triangle has TWO EQUAL SIDES AND TWO EQUAL ANGLES.

Picture an isosceles triangle as an arrow!

A scalene triangle has THREE SIDES OF DIFFERENT LENGTHS and THREE ANGLES OF DIFFERENT sizes.

When picturing a scalene triangle, think of SCALING A MOUNTAIN that has an easy way up or a more difficult side to climb!

Perimeter

Questions on perimeter have caused lots of problems for students in the last few years. We can change that! Let's look at how to calculate the perimeter of a shape.

> **KEY FACT**   • The perimeter is the total distance around the outside of a shape.

The common way of losing marks is to forget one side of a shape when measuring it! Let's do some practice.

Question: **What is the perimeter of this shape?**

1 Read the question then read it again.

What are we being asked to do? **We are being asked to measure the distance around the shape.**

2 Choose a side to start from. Put a line through it with your pencil.

This helps you to remember where you started from.

3 Add up all the lengths that are given in the question. Mark them off as you go.

2 cm + 3 cm + 2 cm + 2 cm + 3 cm + 2 cm + 9 cm = 23 cm

4 Now work out the lengths of the sides you haven't been given.

This is the IMPORTANT PART!
The right angles show you that the distance along the top of the shape must be the same as the distance along the bottom. Both must be **9 cm.**

The missing side must be 3 cm because 3 cm + **3 cm** + 3 cm is **9 cm**

5 Add the missing length to the total of the lengths you have been given (see Step 3).

23 cm + 3 cm = 26 cm

6 Is your answer a sensible one? If so, put it in the box.

The perimeter of the shape is 26 cm.

Tip 1
Think of a perimeter fence going all the way round a football pitch.

Tip 2
If you have to measure with a ruler, make sure you are accurate to the nearest millimetre.

Tip 3
Don't try to measure 'missing' sides with a ruler. The reason they are missing is because the test wants to see if you can work it out from the given lengths.

The 24 Hour Clock

You should be pretty good at telling the time by now but certain questions can still cause problems. It is very easy to make silly mistakes when dealing with the 24 hour clock. When you are working out time it is important to take things step by step.

Let's try a question.

Question: **How long is it from 01:12 to 22:15?**

1 Read the question then read it again.

2 Picture the question.

Imagine the times: 01:12 is very early in the morning; 22:15 is late at night. The answer is going to be quite high.

3 Count the minutes round to the first hour.

01:12 to 02:00 is 48 minutes.

4 Now count the hours round to the given hour.

02:00 to 22:00 is 20 hours.

5 Add up the minutes and convert to hours if you need to.

48 minutes + 15 minutes = 63 minutes.
63 minutes = 1 hour and 3 minutes.

6 Calculate all the hours and add the remaining minutes to give a final answer.

20 hours + 1 hour + 3 minutes = 21 hours and 3 minutes.

7 Does the answer look sensible? If so, put it in the box.

Yes. 21 hours and 3 minutes is correct.

Practice Questions

Work out the following times in hours and minutes.

1   09:46 to 15:38   3   19:41 to 02:27

2   07:28 to 18:55

Tip 1
Get used to reading timetables for buses, trains and aeroplanes. Test yourself on imaginary journeys.

Tip 2
Remember, when comparing times the **fastest** one is the **shortest** one.

Reading Scales

We use scales to measure things. They are just like number lines! The tricky bit is remembering that you need to work out what each mark on the scale stands for.

Let's try a question involving reading scales.

Question: **How much water is there in the measuring cylinder?**

[   ] **ml**

1 Read the question then read it again.

2 Picture the numbers.
The answer is between 150 ml and 200 ml.

3 Study the scale.
Count the gaps made by the small lines between 150 ml and 200 ml. There are 5 gaps. We therefore know that **5 gaps must equal 50 ml.**

4 Calculate the scale.
5 gaps = 50 ml
1 gap = 10 ml (50 ÷ 5)

5 Answer the question.
Water level is at 150 ml plus 2 gaps
= 150 ml + 20 ml
= 170 ml

6 If your answer looks sensible, write it in the box.
If not, go back to Step 2 and try again.

Tip 1
Read scales very carefully and count the gaps more than once to be sure you have got it right. Write in missing measurements in pencil to help you remember them.

Tip 2
Always check your answer carefully to be sure it makes sense.

Venn Diagrams

Venn diagrams may sound complicated but really they are just a way of sorting information into groups. Look at the diagram. There are three regions – A, B and C.

Region A belongs to group A.
Region B belongs to group B.
Region C belongs to group A and group B.

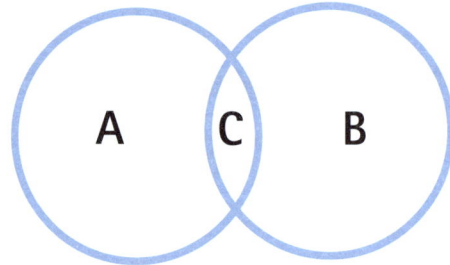

Let's try a typical question.

Question: **Look at this table and sort the names into the sorting diagram. Decide on a description for each region.**

Name	Likes apples	Likes bananas
Mary	✔	✗
Jack	✗	✔
Fabio	✔	✔
Ronnie	✔	✔
Sarah	✔	✗
Gemma	✔	✗
Joshua	✔	✗

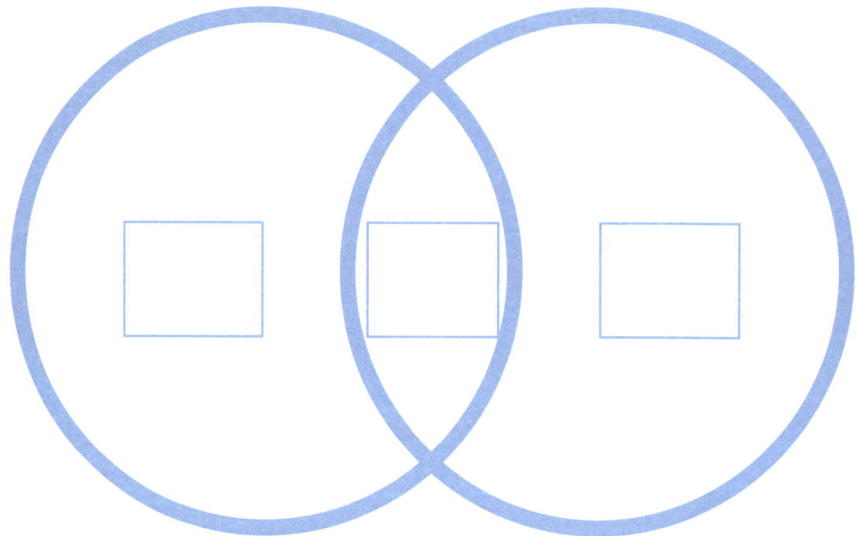

1 Read the question then read it again.

We need to sort the names into groups and decide on definitions or labels for each of these groups.

2 Study the information given.

We can sort the information into two main groups: Group A *(children who like apples)* and Group B *(children who like bananas)*.
Group C will therefore be *children who like apples and bananas.*

3 Sort the information.

Write out the groups on practice paper first.

4 Check your answer against your table.

Check back to make sure you have included all the children in the right groups before completing your answer.

Pictograms

Pictograms are not really tricky but they do sometimes catch us out! With pictograms just remember that PICTURE = NUMBER.

Let's try a question (remember there is always a clue to help you).

Question: **Class 2A sold ice creams at the summer fair to raise money for their school trip.**

How many ice creams did Tom sell? [   ] **ice creams**

Laura	🍦🍦🍦
Tom	🍦🍦🍦
Fred	🍦
Jane	🍦🍦🍦🍦

🍦 = 20 ice creams

1	Read the question then read it again.	This is a pictogram. Look for the clue.
2	What is the clue?	The clue is that 🍦 = 20 ice creams. So 🍦 = 10 ice creams.
3	Study the pictogram.	Tom sold 🍦🍦🍦
4	Calculate your answer.	So Tom sold 20 + 20 + 10 = 50 ice creams.
5	If your answer looks sensible, write it in the box.	If not, go back to Step 2 and start again.

Tip
If there isn't a clue to tell you how much each picture is worth then each picture must equal 1.

Checking Your Answers

INVERSE OPERATIONS

Remember, adding and subtracting are OPPOSITES. Multiplying and dividing are OPPOSITES. We can use this knowledge to check our calculations quickly.

e.g.   75 + 85 = 160   or   42 x 6 = 252
CHECK   160 – 85 = 75   CHECK   252 ÷ 6 = 42

INVERSE means the same as OPPOSITE

Question: **2128 ÷ 28 =**

1 Read the question then read it again.

Divide 2128 by 28

2 Study the numbers. Picture them in your head.

Picture them on a number line.

3 Perform the calculation.

$$\begin{array}{r} 76 \\ 28\overline{)2128} \\ \underline{196} \\ 168 \end{array}$$

4 Does the answer look sensible? If it does then check it using the INVERSE OPERATION.

The opposite of dividing is multiplying so ...

$$\begin{array}{r} 76 \\ X28 \\ \hline 608 \\ 1520 \\ \hline \mathbf{2128} \end{array}$$

5 Does the check answer match the original sum? If it does then enter the answer in the box! If it doesn't then go back to Step 1.

Yes! Our answer is correct!

Practice Questions

Do these calculations and then check your answers using the inverse operation.

1   92 x 36 =

2   471 + 849 =

3   13 662 ÷ 23 =

4   8076 – 591 =

Tip

Get into the habit of checking your answers quickly. This will save time and marks in your test!

ROUNDING UP OR DOWN

Another excellent way to check your answers is to round the numbers in the question up or down. Doing this will give you a simple sum to do and give you a rough answer.

Question: **52 x 28 =** [   ]

1 Read the question then read it again.

$52 \times 28 = ?$

2 Study the numbers. Picture them in your head.

Picture them on a number line.

3 Perform the calculation.

$$\begin{array}{r} 52 \\ \times \quad 28 \\ \hline 416 \\ 1040 \\ \hline \mathbf{1456} \end{array}$$

4 Now round off the numbers and mentally calculate your answer.

52 ROUND TO 50
28 ROUND TO 30
$50 \times 30 = 1500$

5 Are the answers reasonably close? If so then enter your answer in the box. If not then you must go back to Step 1.

Yes, 1456 is pretty close to 1500. Our answer looks correct!

Practice Questions

Do these calculations and then check your answers using the 'Rounding Up or Down' technique.

1   $88 \times 71 =$ [   ]

2   $4607 - 395 =$ [   ]

3   $796 - 507 =$ [   ]

4   $782 \div 17 =$ [   ]

Tip 1
When rounding up or down think of 'friendly' numbers. These are numbers you can work with easily in your head. Some examples are 2, 5, 10, 50, 100 and so on.

Tip 2
Get used to doing mental calculations every day. Give your brain 'gym exercises' to do which involve calculating numbers quickly. Darts can be a fun way to do this!

Multiplying and Dividing by 10, 100 and 1000

At Level 5 you must be able to multiply and divide whole numbers and decimals by 10, 100 and 1000.

Let's try a simple example.

Question: **Write in the missing number.**

4.73 x 10 = ☐

1 Read the question then read it again.

4.73 x 10 =

2 Picture the numbers. What do they look like?

4.73 is nearly 5.

3 Study the numbers again and think about them.

You know the answer should be about 50 (5 x 10 = 50).

4 Remember the rules!

To multiply a decimal by 10 shuffle the numbers **one** place to the left, leaving the decimal point in place.

5 Calculate.

4.73 x 10 – shift the numbers one place to the left.

6 Check your answer.

so   4.73 x 10 = 47.3
            47.3 is nearly 50

7 If your answer looks sensible, write it in the box. If not go back to Step 3.

From Step 3 we know our answer should be about 50. Our answer looks correct!

KEY FACTS – Multiplication

- To multiply a decimal by 100 shuffle the numbers **two** places to the left.

- To multiply a decimal by 1000 shuffle the numbers **three** places to the left.

- Sometimes you will need to add zeros to fill blank spaces.
  e.g.   3.8 x 100 = 380
                2.68 x 1000 = 2680

Tip

When multiplying **whole** numbers by 10, 100 and 1,000 just add the correct number of zeros!

x 10	add 0 to the end	27 x 10 = 270
x 100	add 00 to the end	27 x 100 = 2700
x 1000	add 000 to the end	27 x 1000 = 27 000

Let's try another question. This time we will DIVIDE a decimal number.
(Remember: dividing is the **opposite** of multiplying.)

Question: **Write in the missing number.**

$38.3 \div 10 =$ ▢

1 | Read the question then read it again. | $38.3 \div 10 =$

2 | Picture the numbers. What do they look like? | 38.3 is nearly 40.

3 | Study the numbers again and think about them. | You know the answer should be about 4 $(40 \div 10 = 4)$.

4 | Remember the rules! | To divide a decimal by 10, shuffle the numbers **one** place to the right.

5 | Calculate. | Shift the numbers one place to the right.

6 | Check your answer. | So $38.3 \div 10 = 3.83$
3.83 is nearly 4

7 | If your answer looks sensible, write it in the box. If not go back to Step 3. | From Step 3 we know our answer should be about 4. Our answer looks correct!

KEY FACTS – Division

- To divide a decimal by 100 shuffle the numbers **two** places to the right.

- To divide a decimal by 1000 shuffle the numbers **three** places to the right.

Practice Questions

1 $37 \times 10 =$ ▢

2 $42 \times$ ▢ $= 4200$

3 $0.3 \times 10 =$ ▢

4 $4.6 \div 10 =$ ▢

5 $362 \div$ ▢ $= 36.2$

6 $6500 \div 1000 =$ ▢

Decimals

To achieve Level 5 you must be able to work with numbers to two decimal places. Decimals are easy – remember, money is written with decimals! For example, £9.85 is nearly £10.00; 3.07 is a bit more than 3.

Let's try some questions.

Question: **Write in the missing number.**

3.51 x 4.9 =

1 Read the question then read it again.

3.51 x 4.9 = ?

2 Picture the numbers. What do they look like?

3.51 is around halfway between 3 and 4. 4.9 is just less than 5.

3 Study the numbers again and think about them!

You know the answer is going to be more than 12 (3 x 4) and less than 20 (4 x 5). Remember there is a total of **three** numbers to the right of the decimal points.

4 When multiplying and dividing remove the decimal point and calculate.

```
        351
  X      49
       3159
      14040
      17199
```

5 Check back to your estimate at Step 3.

You know that your number is going to be between 12 and 20 (see Step 3).

6 Replace the decimal point.

Count **three** in from the right (see Step 3). Your answer is 17.199!

7 Round up or down so you only have 2 numbers after the decimal point.

17.199 becomes 17.20 when you round to two decimal places.

8 If your answer looks sensible, write it in the box.

If it doesn't look right, go back to Step 3 and try again.

Tip 1
When rounding, remember 5 is always UP!

1.265 = 1.27

Tip 2
When writing money remember:
£0.45p (X)   £0.45 (✓)
0.45p (X)   45p (✓)
Say the answer to yourself before you write it down!

Here is another 'decimals' question we can try together. There are some questions at the bottom of the page for you to try on your own!

Question: $(6.73 - 4.89) + 1.25 =$ ☐

1 | Read the question then read it again. | $(6.73 - 4.89) + 1.25 = ?$

2 | Picture the numbers. What do they look like? | 6.73 is getting close to 7.
4.89 is nearly 5.
1.25 is a bit more than 1.

3 | Study the numbers again and think about them! | $7 - 5 = 2$
$2 + 1$ and a bit $= 3$ and a bit

4 | Calculate. | Remember – always do the bits in brackets first!

i) $\begin{array}{r} 6.73 \\ -\ 4.89 \\ \hline 1.84 \end{array}$ ii) $\begin{array}{r} 1.84 \\ +\ 1.25 \\ \hline 3.09 \end{array}$

5 | Check back to your estimate at Step 3. | You know that your number is going to be a bit more than 3 (see Step 3 above).

6 | Make sure your decimal point is in the right place. | Your answer is 3.09!

7 | Round up or down so you only have two numbers after the decimal point. | You only have two numbers after the decimal point so you don't need to do anything!

8 | If your answer looks sensible, write it in the box. | If it doesn't – go back to Step 3 and try again.

Practice Questions

Here are some questions for you to try Remember to use the step by step approach above.

1 $(2.3 + 4.75) \times 5.91 =$ ☐

2   £20 – (£4.62 x 3) = ☐

Reducing a Fraction to its Simplest Form

Reducing fractions is all about finding a fraction's 'common factors'. This sounds complicated but is really very simple. For example;

$\frac{4}{6}$ can be reduced to $\frac{2}{3}$ (because 4 and 6 can both be divided by 2)

$\frac{2}{4}$ can be reduced to $\frac{1}{2}$ (because 2 and 4 can both be divided by 2)

Question: **What is $\frac{36}{90}$ in its lowest form?**

1   Read the question then read it again.

2   Are both numbers divisible by 2?
Yes? Then divide them both by 2.
No? Move to Step 4.

Yes $36 \div 2 = 18$
       $90 \div 2 = 45$

3   Look at your new fraction. Can the numbers be divided by 2 again?
Yes? Repeat Step 2.
No? Move to Step 4.

$\frac{18}{45}$

Both numbers cannot be divided by 2 so we move to Step 4.

4   Study the fraction. Which number (other than 1) can be divided into both the top and bottom numbers?

Both 18 and 45 can be divided by 9!

5   Reduce the fraction. Enter your answer in the box.

$18 \div 9 = 2$ $45 \div 9 = 5$

Our answer is $\frac{2}{5}$

Practice Questions

Try these for practice. Reduce each of the fractions to their lowest form:

1 $\frac{14}{42}$ =   **2** $\frac{15}{40}$ =   **3** $\frac{36}{48}$ =   **4** $\frac{32}{56}$ =

Tip 1

Learn to recognise these equivalent fractions. They may help you in your test.

$\frac{1}{3} = \frac{2}{6} = \frac{3}{9} = \frac{4}{12} = \frac{5}{15} = \frac{6}{18} = \frac{7}{21}$

$\frac{1}{4} = \frac{2}{8} = \frac{3}{12} = \frac{4}{16} = \frac{5}{20} = \frac{6}{24} = \frac{7}{28}$

$\frac{1}{5} = \frac{2}{10} = \frac{3}{15} = \frac{4}{20} = \frac{5}{25} = \frac{6}{30} = \frac{7}{35}$

Tip 2

Remember, when you are reducing a fraction ask yourself the following questions **before writing anything down:**
- Which numbers fit?
- How many times do they fit?

You can use your ability to reduce fractions to their lowest form to help you answer questions on **RATIO** and **PROPORTION**.

Have a look at this pattern of squares:

Let's try a question.
Question: **What is the ratio of blue squares to white squares?**

1 Read the question then read it again.

2 Count the number of blue squares. There are 4 blue squares.

3 Now count the white squares. There are 8 white squares.

4 What is the ratio of blue squares to white squares? The ratio is 4:8

5 Can you reduce the ratio? Follow Step 2 to Step 5 on page 20.

6 Write your answer in the box. Write this as a ratio 1:2

KEY FACT

When doing a question about proportion, count the TOTAL number of squares. This can be written as a fraction.

The proportion of blue squares in the pattern at the top of this page is 4 in 12 or $\frac{4}{12}$. Reduce this using the steps on page 20. The proportion of blue squares in the whole pattern is 1 in 3 or $\frac{1}{3}$.

Practice Questions

Look at the pattern below and answer the following questions:

1 What is the ratio of blue squares to white squares?
2 What is the proportion of blue squares in the whole pattern?

Tip

If you are asked to find a **proportion** or **ratio** of two things or numbers you are being asked to find a **fraction** (in its lowest form).

Calculating Fractions or Percentages

Without a Calculator

Lots of questions that ask you to find fractions or percentages of things are easy to answer WITHOUT a calculator by just using some simple maths, such as doubling, halving or dividing by 10. For example:

70% of 900 metres

so

10% of 900 is 90

70% of 900 is 7 x 90

7 x 90 = 630

= 630 metres

Let's try a harder question together.

Question: **A jacket costs £130. In the sales the price is reduced by 15%. What is the new price of the jacket?**

1 Read the question then read it again. What am I being asked to do?

Find the NEW price of the jacket.

2 To find the discount, first calculate 10% of the original price.

10% of £130 = £13.

3 Now calculate 5% of the original price and add your answers together to find 15%.

5% is half of 10% so 5% is £6.50
(5%) + (10%) = (15%)
£6.50 + £13.00 = £19.50

4 Don't forget the next part! What is the NEW price of the jacket?

The jacket has been reduced by £19.50
So the new price is £130 - £19.50 = £110.50

5 Check you have answered the question properly.

What is the new price of the jacket? After discount of £19.50 the new price is **£110.50.**

Tip 1

To find 1% of something, first find 10% then find 10% of THAT answer. You can work out any % by adding all the 10%, 5% and 1% answers together!

Tip 2

Remember as many percentage/fraction equivalents as you can:

$50\% = \frac{1}{2}$ $25\% = \frac{1}{4}$ $75\% = \frac{3}{4}$

$33\% =$ nearly $\frac{1}{3}$ $66\% =$ nearly $\frac{2}{3}$

With a Calculator

You can work out many fractions or percentages very easily without a calculator but sometimes it's not so easy. For example, if you scored 15 out of 30 in your spelling test you should be able to recognise that you got 50% correct. If you improved the following week and got 24 out of 30 then you may need to use your calculator! Calculate as follows:

24   **÷**   **30**   **%**

You should have the answer 80 which means you scored 80% correct.

Let's try another.

Question: **Calculate 51 out of 68 as a percentage.**

1 Read the question then read it again.

51 out of 68 means $\frac{51}{68}$

2 Picture the numbers in your head.

51 out of 68 is nearly 50 out of 70 or $\frac{5}{7}$
Our answer will be somewhere between $\frac{1}{2}$ and 1

3 Type in the numbers.

51   **÷**   **68**

4 Press the % key.

%

5 Does your answer look sensible?
If yes, put your answer in the box.

Our answer is 75%. Remember it only takes a moment to redo the calculation as a check!

Practice Questions Work these out **without** a calculator.

1 75% of 500 cm

2 40% of 160 kg

3 35% of £260

4 65% of 800 ml

Practice Questions Work these out **with** a calculator (express them as a %).

1 $\frac{48}{150}$

2 $\frac{77}{220}$

3 $\frac{65}{500}$

Multiplication and Division

To get a Level 5 you need to be able to multiply and divide a 3 digit number by a 2 digit number without a calculator! EASY!

Question: **Write in the missing number.**

217 x 48 = ☐

1 Read the question then read it again.

217 x 48 =

2 Picture the numbers.

217 is close to 200.
48 is close to 50.

3 Study the numbers and think about them.

217 x 48 is approximately 200 x 50 = 10 000

4 Calculate your answer.

```
      217
  x    48
     1736  (217 x 8)
     8680  (217 x 40)
    10416
```

5 Does your answer look sensible? If it does then write it in the box. If it doesn't then go back to Step 3.

10 416 is close to 10 000 (see Step 3). Our answer looks sensible!

Question: **Write in the missing number. 587 x 32 =** ☐

1 Read the question then read it again.

587 x 32 =

2 Picture the numbers.

587 is close to 600.
32 is close to 30.

3 Study the numbers and think about them.

587 x 32 is approximately 600 x 30 = 18 000

4 Calculate your answer.

```
      587
  x    32
     1174      (587 x 2)
    17610      (587 x 30)
    18784
```

5 Does your answer look sensible? If it does then write it in the box. If it doesn't then go back to Step 3.

18 784 is approximately 18 000 (see Step 3). Our answer looks sensible.

Now let's try division!

Question: **Write in the missing number. 917 ÷ 12 =** ⬚

1 Read the question then read it again.

917 ÷ 12 =

2 Picture the numbers – what do they look like?

917 is close to 900.
12 is close to 10.

3 Study the numbers and think about them.

917 ÷ 12 is approximately 900 ÷ 10 = 90

4 Calculate your answer.

```
        76.4
12 ) 917
       84
       77
       72
       50
       48
```

5 If your answer looks sensible, write it in the box.

Our answer (to one decimal place) is 76.4.

Key fact x and ÷ are opposites.
Use this fact to help with tricky questions.

21 x 16 = 336   336 ÷ 21 = 16

16 x ⬚ = 336 **so** 336 ÷ 16 = 21   **Our missing number is 21.**

Practice Questions
Try these for practice.

1 486 ÷ 27 = ⬚   **2** 852 ÷ 12 = ⬚   **3** 744 ÷ ⬚ = 24

4 361 x 35 = ⬚   **5** 792 x 83 = ⬚   **6** 457 x ⬚ = 5484

Tip
Be neat. Keep
your numbers
in the right
columns.

```
   WRONG
      312
x      14
     3120
     1248
     4368
```

```
   RIGHT
      312
x      14
     3120
     1248
     4368
```

Negative Numbers

Be positive! NEGATIVE NUMBERS ARE EASY. Imagine a thermometer and you have a number line with positive and negative numbers. So chill out and try this question.

Question: **Put these temperatures in order from coldest to warmest:**

$$-8°, -20°, -3°, 18°, 30°, 6°, -10°$$

1 Read the question then read it again.

Negative numbers are colder than positive numbers.

2 Picture the numbers.

Group the numbers.
Negative: (-8°, -20°, -3°, -10°)
Positive: (18°, 30°, 6°)

3 Study the numbers.

Draw a number line. Don't forget to include 'zero'. Decide where each number goes.

| -20° | | -10° -8° | -3° 0° | 6° | | 18° | | 30° |

4 Check your answer.

Are the numbers in order?
Check you have used every number.

5 If your answer looks sensible, write it in the box.

If not go back to Step 3 and try again.

Tip 1

Numbers are often called **INTEGERS**. Don't let this put you off. This just means WHOLE numbers without decimals!

These are integers   1, 2, 3, 4

These are **not integers**   5.6, 7.8, 11.3

Tip 2

When thinking of negative (–) numbers – think of a ladder going into a hole in the ground.
-2 is higher than -6
-5 is below -4

Try another question. This time it's a word problem.

Question: **The temperature is –6°. It rises by 9°.**

What is the new temperature?

1 Read the question then read it again.

2 Picture the numbers.

3 Calculate your answer.

4 Check your answer.

5 If your answer checks out, write it in the box.

Rises means **getting warmer**.

-6° is colder than 9°.

-9 -8 -7 -6 -5 -4 -3 -2 -1 0 1 2 3 4 5 6 7 8 9 10

The temperature starts at -6°. We then need to count up 9 places.

Did you count in the right direction? When **adding** to a negative number always count to the right on a number line.

Our answer is 3° which is 9° warmer than -6°!

Practice Questions

1 Put these temperatures in order, lowest to highest:

-2°, 3°, 0°,

-5°, -7°

2 Order these integers correctly starting with the smallest:

-43, -21, 17, 6, -35

3 At 8am the temperature is -2°. It falls by 3° every hour. What will the temperature be at 3pm?

4 On Tuesday the temperature was -3°. On Wednesday the temperature was 12°. What is the difference between Tuesday's and Wednesday's temperatures?

Simple Formulae

Formulae can be written in words or in letters. To achieve Level 5 you may be required to make up your own formulae in the tests. This is easier than it sounds! Let's start by working through this example.

Question: **Here is a formula for finding the total cost of some computer games.**

$$T = £15 \times N$$

T = total cost   Each game costs £15   N = number of games

Now write a formula for finding the cost of one game when the total cost of N games is £135 and the cost of one game is C.

1 | Read the question then read it again. | Lots to read and think about here!

2 | What am I being asked to do? | Write a formula for finding the cost of one game using £135 and 'N'.

3 | It will help if you say the formula to yourself. | The total cost is the cost of one game, C, multiplied by the total number of games, N. So...
The cost of one game is the total cost, £135, **divided** by the total number of games.

4 | Change your logical statement into a simple formula. Say it to yourself when you write it down. | The cost of one game...   C
...is the total cost...   £135
...divided by ($\div$) the total number of games N

$C = 135 \div N$ **OR**
$C = \dfrac{135}{N}$

Tip 1
• Talk through your formula in your head.
• Think clearly.
• Take it step by step.

Tip 2
Only use letters that relate to the information in the question.

A simple formula is often used to find out the total cost of items bought.
In words this formula can be written:

"The total cost is the cost for one item multiplied by the number of those items bought."

In letter formulae this could be written as: $T = N \times P$

T = total cost   P = cost of each item   N = number of items bought

Practice Questions

Use the $T = N \times P$ formula to work out these questions.

1 What is the value of **T** if **N** = 6 and **P** = £1.50?

2 What is the value of **N** if **T** = £20 and **P** = £4?

3 What is the value of **P** if **T** = £36 and **N** = 2?

Example Question

Andrea and Jamie are playing a number game. Jamie
gives Andrea a number which she changes using a rule:
"I take Jamie's number and multiply it by 7 then subtract 2."
Write a formula to show the process Andrea goes through to get to her answer.
Use J for Jamie's number and A for Andrea's answer.

$A = (J \times 7) - 2$

Practice Question

Now Andrea changes the rule:
"I take Jamie's number and multiply it by 5 then add 4."
Write a formula to show the process Andrea goes through to get to her answer.
Use J for Jamie's number and A for Andrea's answer.

A =

Tip
If a number and a letter are next to each other,
e.g. 4N, it means they are multiplied. Why is the
x (multiply) symbol left out? It could get confused
with the letter x!!

Using Brackets

To achieve Level 5 in Maths you must be able to answer questions that contain brackets. Let's look at a simple example.

Firstly, a sum without brackets might look like this:

$2 + 2 \times 5 + 7 = 27$

If brackets are used then the answer changes:

$(2 + 2) \times (5 + 7) = 48$

CALCULATIONS INSIDE BRACKETS MUST BE DONE FIRST!
Our second example actually becomes $4 \times 12 = 48$ when we calculate the brackets first.

Let's try a harder question.

Question: $(673 - 489) \div 23 = $ ☐

1 Read the question then read it again.

$(673 - 489) \div 23 = ?$

2 Picture the numbers. What do they look like?

Picture them on a number line.

3 Calculate the numbers in the brackets first. Check your answer to see if it's sensible.

$$\begin{array}{r} 673 \\ -\ 489 \\ \hline 184 \end{array}$$

4 Complete the calculation and enter your answer.

$$\begin{array}{r} 8 \\ 23\overline{)184} \\ 184 \end{array}$$

Tip
Brackets are very sensitive and need your attention.

ALWAYS CALCULATE THE BRACKETS FIRST!

Here is another question with brackets that we can do together. Try the practice questions at the bottom when you think you're ready.

Question: $\dfrac{(48 \times 4) + (154 \times 2)}{20}$ = [ ]

1 Read the question then read it again.

$\dfrac{(48 \times 4) + (154 \times 2)}{20}$ = ?

2 Picture the numbers. What do they look like?

Picture them on a number line. Is this a big number?

3 Calculate the numbers in the brackets first.

i)
```
   48
X   4
  192
```
ii)
```
  154
X   2
  308
```

4 Complete the calculation and then enter the answer.

192 + 308 = **500** then

```
      25
20 |500
   40
   100
```

Practice Questions

Here are some questions for you to try. Remember to use the step by step approach above.

1 78 x (97 + 42) = [ ]

2 (41 x 76) + [ ] = 4000

3 (14 x 60) + [ ] = 850

4 $\dfrac{(57 \times 6) - (41 \times 7)}{5}$ = [ ]

Coordinates

To achieve Level 5 you should be familiar with **coordinates and quadrants**. Let's try a question to practise what we know!

Question: **Write down the coordinates of each point on this graph.**

1st quadrant	=	(_ , _)
2nd quadrant	=	(_ , _)
3rd quadrant	=	(_ , _)
4th quadrant	=	(_ , _)

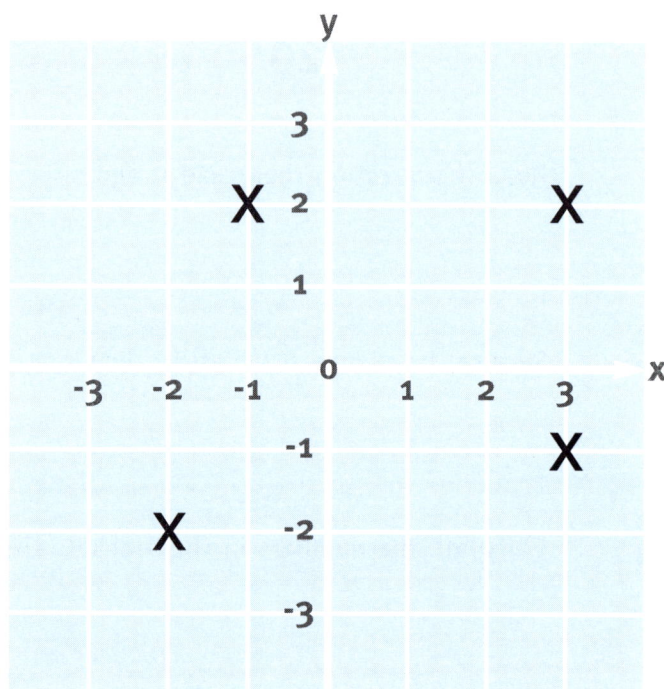

1 Read the question then read it again.

2 Practise your answer.

You can sketch in lines to help you read the coordinates.

3 Check the number of each quadrant.

2nd quadrant | 1st quadrant

3rd quadrant | 4th quadrant

4 Read off the coordinates in each quadrant.

Remember:
ALONG the x axis first then **UP** or **DOWN** the y axis
1 (3, 2)   **2** (-1, 2)
3 (-2, -2)   **4** (3, -1)

5 Double–check and write in your answer.

Check twice! Write once!

Let's try another question.

Question: **Draw a reflection of the pentagon in the x axis. Record the coordinates of each vertex.**

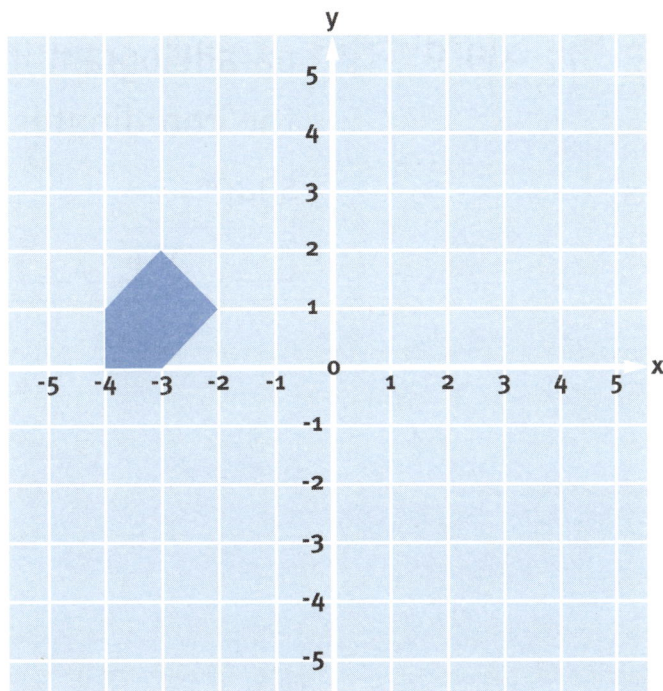

(___ , ___)   (___ , ___)   (___ , ___)   (___ , ___)   (___ , ___)

1 Read the question then read it again.

Note you are being asked to work in the 3rd quadrant. **'vertex = corner'**

2 Practise your answer.

Sketch your pentagon on rough paper first.

3 Note the position of your shape.

Remember your pentagon must go in the 3rd quadrant!

4 Draw your shape on the grid.

5 Read off your coordinates.

Remember **ALONG** then **UP/DOWN**
(–4, 0), (–4, –1), (–3, –2), (–2, –1), (–3, 0)

6 Double-check and write in the answer.

Check twice! Write once!

Practice Questions

1 In which quadrants will we find:

(–3, –2)?   (–2, 1)?   (1, 3)?

[ ]   [ ]   [ ]

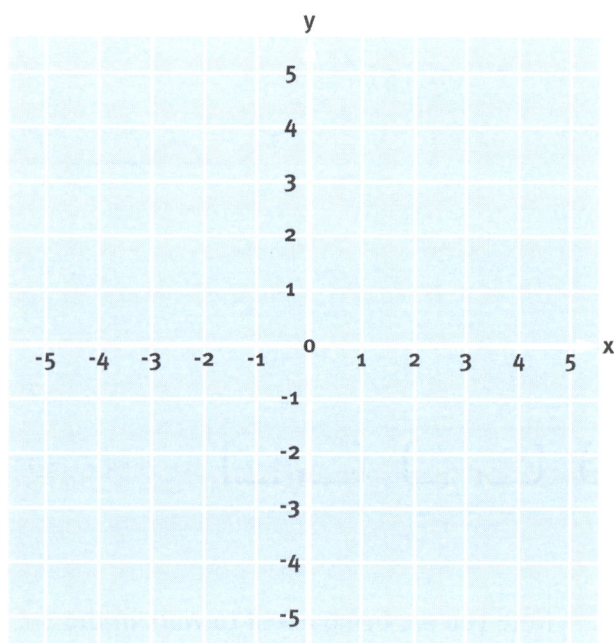

2 Draw a reflection of the parallelogram in the x axis. Name the coordinates of the reflected shape.

(__ , __) (__ , __) (__ , __) (__ , __)

Tip 1

Coordinates always go ALONG the corridor and UP the stairs

But sir, you can go DOWN stairs as well!

Always go along first when reading coordinates or.... x (axis) comes before y (axis)!!!

Tip 2

Coordinates are always written in brackets.
(3, 4)   (–3, –2)
or
(x axis, y axis)

Angles

To achieve Level 5 you will need to be able to measure and draw angles and use the correct language for them. **Don't worry** if you need to measure angles, you will be given a protractor or an angle measurer in the test.

Measuring Angles

Question: **Use an angle measurer or a protractor to measure these angles.**

1 Read the question then read it again.

2 Use the curved line to help you find the angle you need to measure.

Where will you measure? Use the curved line to help you.

3 Study the angles.

Estimate and label the angles to help you check your answers:

(a) is an **acute angle** – less than 90°.
(b) is an **obtuse angle** – more than 90° and less than 180°.
(c) is a **reflex angle** – more than 180° and less than 360°.

4 Measure the angles.

Match up the angle measurer and the lines carefully.

5 Check your answers against your estimates in Step 3.

Does each answer match your estimate?

6 If your answer looks sensible, write it in the box.

If not, go back to Step 3 and try again.

Drawing Angles

Let's try drawing some angles. Use some paper to practise.

Question: **Use an angle measurer or a protractor to draw these angles to the nearest degree.**

(a) 53°   (b) 87°   (c) 142°

1 Read the question then read it again.

2 Study the angles.

Label the angles to help you:

(a) an **acute angle** – less than 90°.
(b) an **acute angle** – less than 90°.
(c) an **obtuse angle** – between 90° and 180°.

3 Measure the angles.

Draw your first line (along the page).
Then measure the angle you need.

4 Check your answers against your estimates in Step 2.

Does each answer match your estimate?

To achieve Level 5 you also need to be able to measure or work out the size of the angles in a triangle and at a point.

Question: **Find the missing angle in this triangle.**

60° 75°

1	**Read the question then read it again.**	We are given two angles. We need to work out the missing angle.
2	**Picture the shape and remember the formula.**	Angles in a triangle add up to 180°.
3	**Study the numbers.**	You know two angles so you can work out the **third**.
4	**Calculate your answer.**	60° + 75° = 135° 180° − 135° = 45°
5	**Check your answer.**	Add the three angles together: 60° + 75° + 45° = 180°
6	**If your answer checks out, write it in the box.**	If not, return to Step 3.

Tip 1
Always turn the paper to make the angles easier to measure. Keep your measurer straight!

Make sure you read the correct scale.

90

180   0

Tip 2
Think of a darts board to help you remember the angles in a triangle.

One hundred and EIGHTYYYYY!

Angles at a Point

Let's try a question together.

Question: **Calculate the angle at this point.**

35°   ?

1	Read the question then read it again.	Calculate usually means you need to do a sum to work out the answer!
2	Picture the shape. Estimate the angle.	The angle is between 180° and 360°
3	Remember the formula.	A complete turn = 360°
4	Study the numbers.	You know one angle so you can work out the other.
5	Calculate your answer.	360° – 35° = 325°
6	Check your answer.	Does it match your estimate?
7	If your answer checks out, write it in the box.	If not, return to Step 4.

Tip 1
A complete turn = 360°
Imagine a skateboarder turning right around.

Tip 2
A right angle is always shown by a box.

Practice Questions

1 Find the missing angles in these triangles.

(a)

75°

(b)

100°

30°

(c)

85°   23°

2 Find the angle at each point.

(a)

?   72°

(b)

110°

?

(c)

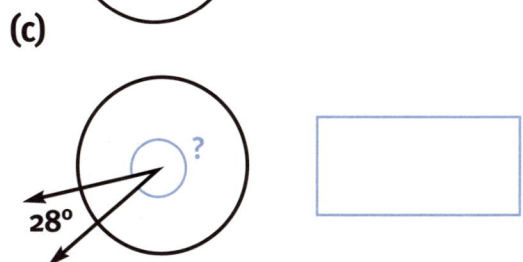

?

28°

3 Estimate the size of these angles. Then label them acute, reflex, obtuse or right.

(a)   **(b)**

(c)   **(d)**

(a)

(b)

(c)

(d)

4 Draw an angle of 85° to the nearest degree.

5 Measure this angle to the nearest degree.

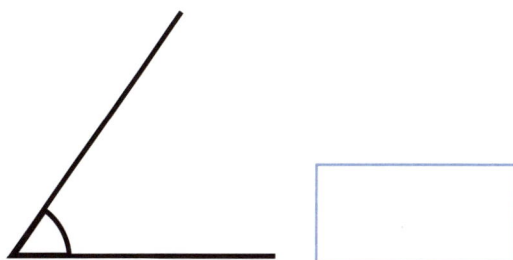

Symmetries of 2D Shapes

To achieve Level 5 in Maths you will need to answer questions on REFLECTION, ROTATION and TRANSLATION in the test.

Let's try some questions that you might come across.

Mirror line

Question: **Draw the reflection of this shape in the mirror line.**

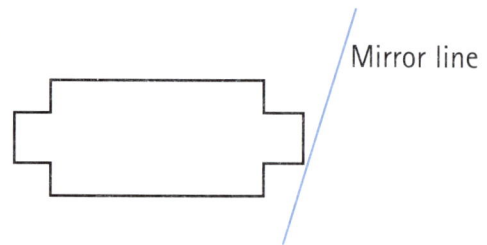

1 Read the question then read it again.

2 Practise your answer.

Trace the shape and the mirror line onto practice paper.

3 Now complete the reflection.

Draw in the reflected shape on your piece of paper.

4 Test your answer.

Fold your paper. Does it work?

5 If it looks right, draw in your answer.

If not, go back to Step 3.

Question: **Does this shape have rotational symmetry?**

1 Read the question then read it again.

2 Practise your answer.

Trace the shape.

3 Test your answer.

Rotate the shape 360°. Does the shape look the same in any other position?

0°   90°   180°   270°

4 Check your answer and write it in.

Yes. The shape looks the same as it does at the start when it is turned around 180 degrees! The shape **does** have rotational symmetry.

Let's try a question about translation now.

Question: **Sketch the position of the shape after a translation of 3 squares right and 4 squares down.**

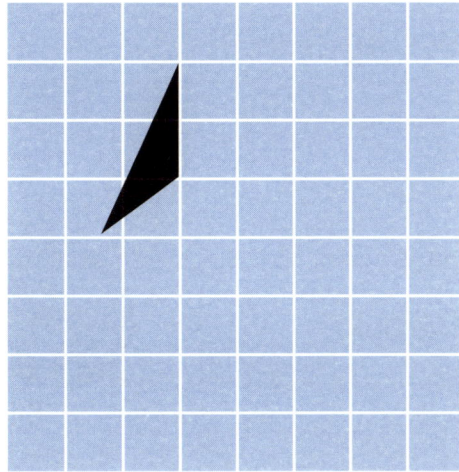

1 | Read the question then read it again.

'translation' = slide along.

2 | Practise your answer.

Trace the shape and practise before you write in your answer.

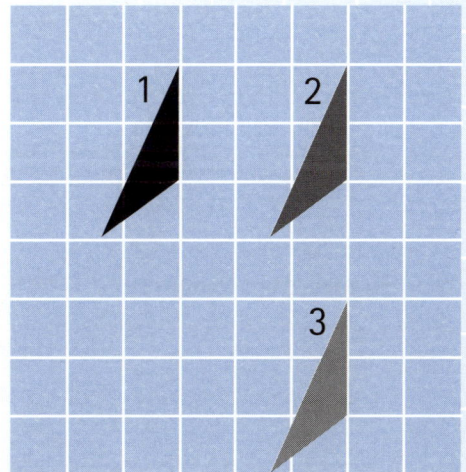

3 | Draw in your final answer.

Double-check first.

Tip
If there is no grid given then trace the object and give it a base.

More About Symmetries

Practice Questions

1 Draw the reflections of these shapes.

2 Which of these shapes have rotational symmetry? Tick those that do.

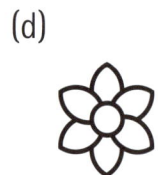

(a)   (b)   (c)   (d)

X   T

Practice Questions

3 Tick the correctly translated shapes.

(a)

(b)

(c)

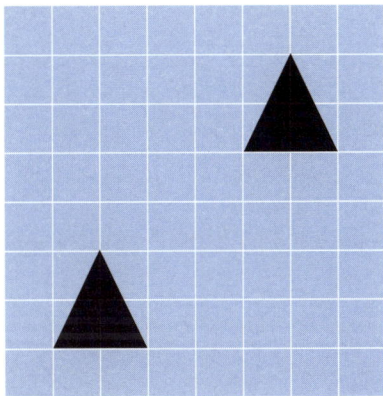

Tip 1
Lines of symmetry = Mirror lines

Tip 2
Don't let your paper slip!

Units of Measure

Comparing Metric to Imperial Units of Measure

To achieve Level 5 you will have to answer questions that ask you to compare Metric units of measurement (kilometres, grams, litres and centimetres) with Imperial units of measurement (miles, pounds, pints). Just remember the equivalence and try this question.

Question: **You run 3 km to school each morning and 3 km home each evening. Approximately how many miles do you run each day?**

1 Read the question then read it again.

3 km x 2 times a day = how many miles?

2 Study the units.

You run 6 km each day.
1 km is about 1.5 miles.

3 Calculate the answer.

6 x 1.5 = 9

4 Remember the units you need for the answer.

9 miles

5 If your answer looks sensible, write it in the box.

If not, go back to Step 2 and try again.

Practice Questions

Here are some questions. Use the Key Facts on page 59 to help you.

1 Approximately how many kilograms is 5 lbs of apples?

kg

2 I drink 1 litre of milk a day. How many **pints** of milk should I order from the milkman for a week?

Tip
Revision Rhymes!

A metre is just 3 feet 3,
It's longer than a yard you see!

2 and a bit pounds of jam is round
about 1 kilo of ham!

To achieve Level 5 you will have to answer questions that ask you to convert one metric unit to another metric unit.

Try this one.

Question: **Write 6.5 km as metres.**

1 Read the question then read it again.   6.5 km = ? metres

2 Study the units.   1 km = 1000 metres

3 Calculate the answer.   6.5 x 1000 = 6500

4 Add in the correct units.   6500 metres

5 If your answer looks sensible, write it in the box.   If not, go back to Step 2 and try again.

Practice Questions
Try some more questions.

1 The weight of my dog is 2.5 kg. What does he weigh in grams?

2 If I drink 1330 ml of water on Saturday and another 1330 ml on Sunday, how much water did I drink altogether?
Circle the correct answer.

(a) 8 litres

(b) 2.66 litres

(c) 13.30 litres

Tip 1
Make up some of your own questions to help you to compare units.

What would you prefer, 1 litre or 1000 ml of cola?

Tip 2
Measure things around you to get a feel for the different units.

g   or   kg

m

Estimating Measures

To achieve Level 5 you will have to estimate measures accurately. This mainly involves using common sense though, so don't worry. You will just need to think about length, weight and quantity in different amounts. These three questions are examples. The notes should help you with estimating.

Question: **Suggest things you would measure in kilometres, metres, centimetres and millimetres.**

- **Kilometres** Anything or anywhere that is too far to walk! For example: the distance to the moon.

- **Metres** Anything or anywhere that you could walk to or around. For example: the garden, playground or bedroom.

- **Centimetres** Anything you could step over. For example: books, TVs or cereal packets.

- **Millimetres** Anything you could step on and squash! For example: ants, Smarties or peanuts.

Question: **Suggest things you would measure in tonnes, kilograms and grams.**

- **Tonnes** Anything you and your friends couldn't lift. For example: a ship, an aeroplane or an elephant!

- **Kilograms** Anything you and an adult could lift. For example: a table, your friend, the sofa.

- **Grams** Anything you could hold in the palm of your hand. For example: a gerbil, a tennis ball.

Question: **Suggest things you would measure in litres, centilitres and millilitres.**

- **Litres** Anything that is too much for you to drink. For example: the bath, a swimming pool.

- **Centilitres** Anything you might drink if you were thirsty. For example: a mug of tea, a glass of milk.

- **Millilitres** Anything that is just a mouthful. For example: a teaspoon of medicine, a sachet of ketchup.

Tip

Get used to thinking about measures and remember a few standard ones to compare against others:

100 m = the length of a football pitch
1 kg = a bag of sugar
1 litre = a carton of juice

Then think about these:

50 m = $\frac{1}{2}$ the length of a football pitch
20 kg = 20 bags of sugar
100 litres = 100 cartons of juice

Practice Questions

1 Estimate the lengths of the following items. Then measure them. Include the unit of measurement you are using.

Item	Estimated Length (with unit)	Actual Length (with unit)
(a) Your Maths Book		
(b) Your Table		
(c) Your Classroom		
(d) Your Playground		

2 Which unit of measurement would you use to measure the following?

(a) The weight of a microwave oven

(b) The distance from London to Paris

(c) The amount of water in a garden pond

(d) The weight of an egg

(e) The length of a grain of rice

(f) The amount of cola in a glass

(g) The weight of a double-decker bus

(h) The length of a tennis court

(i) The amount of juice squeezed from an orange

KEY FACTS – Measures

You may get a question such as this in your test:

Question: **Suggest how you could measure the thickness of one sheet of paper.**

This question is trying to catch you out but don't worry! All you have to do is to measure a large pile of paper and divide the total thickness by the number of pieces of paper in the pile.

So

100 sheets of paper = 75 mm thick
75 ÷ 100 = 0.75 mm

Each sheet of paper is 0.75 mm thick

The Area of a Rectangle

Hurray! There is an easy way to remember how to answer questions about the area of rectangles. Just remember this formula:

Area of a rectangle = the length x the width

Try this question.

Question: **Find the area of this rectangle.**

50 cm

29 cm

1   Read the question then read it again.   TAKE NOTE: you are working with AREA – you need a formula!

2   Remember your formula.   The area of a rectangle = the length x the width

3   Picture the numbers. What do they look like?   29 cm is almost 30 cm. Use this to estimate the answer.

4   Study the numbers again and think about them.   You can estimate that the answer should be around 1500. (50 x 30 = 1500)

5   Calculate your answer.

$$
\begin{array}{r}
50 \\
\times \quad 29 \\
\hline
450 \\
1000 \\
\hline
\mathbf{1450}
\end{array}
$$

6   Add in your unit of measurement.   cm squared (cm^2)

7   Check your answer against your estimate at Step 4.   1450 is close to 1500.

8   If your answer looks sensible, write it in the box.   If not, go back to Step 4 and try again.

Tip 1

When dealing with area, make sure the units are ALWAYS squared.

e.g. cm^2 m^2 km^2

Tip 2

Break up complicated shapes into smaller rectangles to make the question easier to answer. Remember to add up the areas of **all** the rectangles to get your answer!

Let's try another question. Here is a shape you will have to divide up into smaller shapes. Don't be afraid to draw on the test paper.

Question: **Find the area of this shape.**

1 Read the question then read it again.

Look for the key words: **area** and **shape**.

2 Picture the shape.

It looks like two rectangles joined together!

3 Remember the formula.

The area of a rectangle = the length x the width.
We need to measure **two** rectangles.

4 Find the areas of the two rectangles.
Then add them together.

20 x 10 = 200
5 x 3 = 15
Total = 215

5 Add in your unit of measurement.

215 cm²

6 If your answer looks sensible, write it in the box.

If not, go back to Step 4 and try again.

Practice Questions

1 Find the area of this shape.

2 Find the area of this shape.

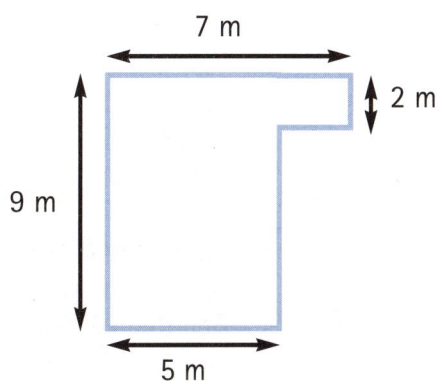

Finding the Mean

Mean data is not 'nasty data'! You will need to be able to find the **mean** of a group of figures to achieve Level 5. Let's try a question.

Question: **Find the mean of these lengths.**

60 cm   28 cm   24 cm   51 cm   17 cm

1 Read the question then read it again.

'mean' = average

2 Think about the question.

Mean – add up the group of numbers and divide by how many numbers there are in the group.

3 Study the numbers.

You know your answer will be less than 60 cm (the longest) and more than 17 cm (the shortest). There are 5 different lengths.

4 Calculate your answer.

60 + 28 + 24 + 51 + 17 = 180
180 ÷ 5 = 36

5 Add in the unit of measurement.

36 cm

6 If your answer looks sensible, write it in the box.

If not, go back to Step 3 and try again.

Practice Questions

Find the mean of these sets of numbers.

1   7, 7, 3, 4, 5, 10   **2** 25, 34, 36, 21, 18, 10

Tip

To find the mean:

Think about sweets! Don't be MEAN!
Share your sweets fairly!
Add them all up then divide them equally!

Finding the Median

To achieve a Level 5 you will need to be able to find the **median** of a group of figures too.

Question: **Look at these temperatures and find the median.**

30°C,   10°C,   –4°C,   12°C,   28°C,   23°C,   15°C

1 Read the question then read it again.

2 Think about the question.

Median is the **middle** number in the group.

○ ○ ○ ○ ○ ○ ○

3 Picture the numbers.

Put them in order from lowest to highest:
–4, 10, 12, 15, 23, 28, 30

4 Study the numbers and work out the answer.

15 is the middle number in this set of numbers.

5 Add in the unit of measurement.

15°C

6 If your answer looks sensible, write it in the box.

If not, go back to Step 4 and try again.

Practice Questions

These are the ages of everyone in my family:
36 years, 7 years, 21 years, 10 years, 42 years.

What is the median age?

Tip

To remember **Median** think **Medium**

Small   **Medium**   Large

(Median is in the middle!)

Finding the Range

To achieve Level 5 you will need to find the **range** of a series of data. Let's try a question.

Question: **These are the times 4 children take to get to school each day:**

20 minutes, 1hour and 30 minutes,

1 hour and 35 minutes, 45 minutes.

What is the range of these times?

1	Read the question then read it again.	
2	Think about the question.	The **range** is the difference between the **lowest** and **highest** value.
3	Picture the numbers.	Put them in order: 20, 45, 1hr 30 and 1hr 35.
4	Study the numbers.	The longest time is 1 hour 35 minutes. The shortest time is 20 minutes. What is the difference between these times?
5	Calculate your answer.	1hr 35 minutes − 20 minutes = 1hr 15 minutes
6	If your answer looks sensible, write it in the box.	If not, go back to Step 3 and try again.

Practice Question

London Zoo has many visitors. What was the range of visitors for the 1st half of last year?

2001

January	20 311	February	28 700	March	56 462
April	15 000	May	34 225	June	62 879

Tip
When calculating the range ALWAYS write down the numbers again, in order of size.

Finding the Mode

Your test might also contain questions on **mode**. Let's try a question.

Question: **These are the results of the red group's maths test:**

65, 65, 80, 72, 80, 80, 91

1 Read the question then read it again.

2 Think about the question.

The **mode** is another name for the **most common value**.

3 Picture the numbers.

Make sets of the same number.

| 65 65 | 72 | 80 80 80 | 91 |

4 Double-check.

Make sure you haven't missed any numbers.

5 Decide on your answer.

80 occurs most often.
80 **is the mode**.

6 If your answer looks sensible, write it in the box.

If not, go back to Step 3 and try again.

Practice Question

The children in Class 4 gave marks out of 10 for a particular television programme. These were the marks given:

6.5,   8.9,   3.9,   8.9,   7.2,   3.5,   6.5,   3.9,   6.5,   4.9,   7.2,   4.9,   8.9,

6.5,   3.9,   3.5,   6.5,   7.2,   8.9,   6.5

What was the modal mark? Modal mark =

Tip 1

Remember:
Mode is the **Most** Common Value
Modal means **Mode**

Tip 2

Always write out the numbers again and sort them. Tick off each number so you know you haven't missed any of them. **This is IMPORTANT!**

Graphs and Pie Charts

To get a Level 5 you will need to look at graphs like the one below and answer questions about them.

Let's try to answer this question using the step by step approach.

Question: **These road signs are in miles. Use the conversion graph to rewrite the road signs in kilometres.**

Dover 15 miles

Canterbury 35 miles

Hastings 45 miles

Dover [   ] km

Canterbury [   ] km

Hastings [   ] km

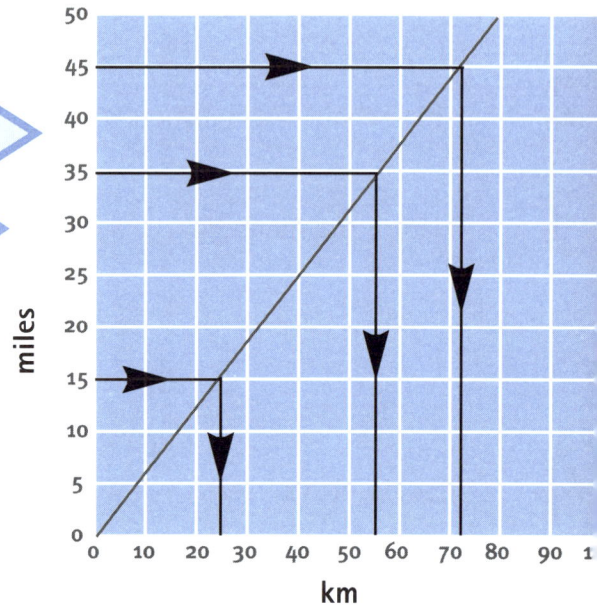

1 | Read the question then read it again. | Conversion graph tells us that we need to convert values.

2 | Be methodical. |

Dover
- We need to change 15 miles into kilometres.
- Go up the y axis (miles) and find 15 (halfway between 10 and 20).
- Mark this point on the y axis with your pencil.
- Go across to the conversion line and make another mark.
- Now go down to find out the value in kilometres.

Our answer is 25!

Now repeat for Canterbury and Hastings.

3 | Does the answer look sensible? If so, fill in the answer box. | Check your answers carefully on the graph before writing them in the boxes. The test marker is looking for an EXACT answer.

Pie charts are a way of showing ideas as a fraction, percentage or proportion. They are an excellent way of showing information quickly and clearly... as long as you know what to look for!

Here are a few to remember:

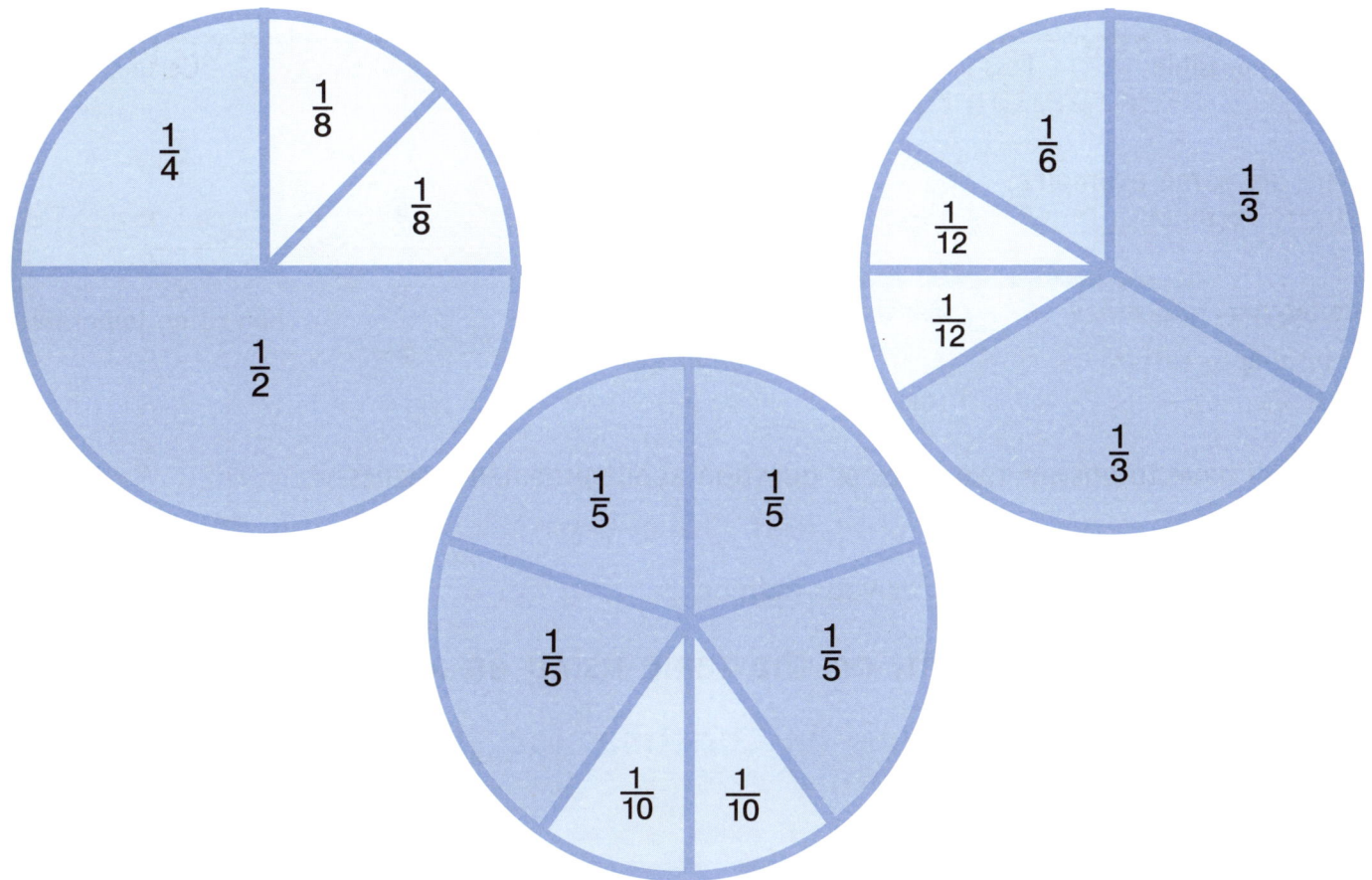

Practice Question

The tourist rate for Japan is 200 yen to £1.00. Draw a graph to convert pounds to yen. Use the graph to find out how much you would receive when you exchange:

(a) £17 = [   ] yen   (b) £24.50 = £ [   ]

(c) 700 yen = £ [   ]   (d) 1350 yen = £ [   ]

Tip 1

Be VERY careful when reading scales or axes. You may be asked to find values BETWEEN lines on the scale. The test marker wants to know if you can find the EXACT answer.

Tip 2

Always draw graphs and read graphs carefully and accurately.
A sharp pencil, straight ruler and steady hand are essential!!

The Probability Scale

The probability scale is a way of showing how likely something is to happen on a scale of 0 to 1.

0	$\frac{1}{4}$	$\frac{1}{2}$	$\frac{3}{4}$	1
Impossible	Less likely	Even chance	More likely	Certain

Here are some examples:

0	$\frac{1}{4}$	$\frac{1}{2}$	$\frac{3}{4}$	1
Pacific Ocean turning to custard		Coin landing on heads		Sun rising tomorrow

You will have to answer two types of question about probability scales.

Let's try a question that asks for your opinion.

Place this statement on the scale using an arrow and a label.

'It will snow on Christmas Day this year.'

0	$\frac{1}{4}$	$\frac{1}{2}$	$\frac{3}{4}$	1
Impossible	Less likely	Even chance	More likely	Certain

1 Read the question then read it again.

Important here as there are more words than numbers!

2 Picture the question in your mind.

Try to imagine snow on Christmas Day. Your first thought might be: 'Yes that is likely because it's cold and Christmas is in winter.'

3 Picture the question again.

Can you remember any white Christmases? If you can then it is probably more likely. If not, then it's probably less likely.

4 Does the answer look sensible? If so, place your arrow on the scale.

Place your arrow on the scale pointing towards 'less likely'.

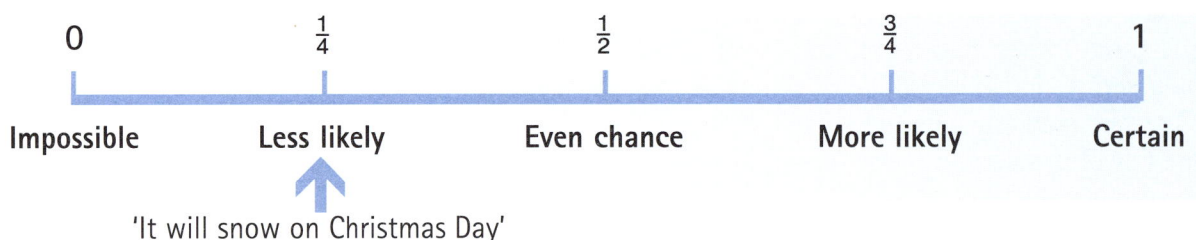

0	$\frac{1}{4}$	$\frac{1}{2}$	$\frac{3}{4}$	1
Impossible	Less likely	Even chance	More likely	Certain

↑
'It will snow on Christmas Day'

Now let's try a probability question that asks for a mathematically correct answer.

These coloured balls were placed in a bag:

12 Red   1 Green   5 Orange   2 Blue

Estimate the chance that the first ball to be taken out of the bag will be an orange ball and mark it on the probability scale.

1 Read the question then read it again.

Words and numbers to think about. What is the question asking you to do?

2 Picture the question in your mind.

Try to picture the different coloured balls going into the bag.

3 Add up the total number of balls.

12 + 1 + 5 + 2 = 20

4 How many of them are orange?

There are 5 orange balls.
So there are 5 orange balls out of 20.

5 Express your probability as a fraction, decimal or percentage. **This is important!**

This can be expressed as

$\frac{1}{4}$ 25%   0.25

6 Decide where to place your arrow.

Draw the arrow a quarter of the way along the line. Be accurate here because the probability scale is clearly marked.

0	$\frac{1}{4}$	$\frac{1}{2}$	$\frac{3}{4}$	1
Impossible	Less likely	Even chance	More likely	Certain

First ball will be orange

Practice Questions

1 There are 24 beads in a bag. 6 are green, 6 are purple, 4 are brown and the rest are blue. What are the chances of taking out a blue bead?

(a) Write your answer down as a fraction, decimal or percentage.

(b) Draw an arrow on a probability scale as an estimate.

Tip 1
When throwing a dice there is an EQUAL chance of rolling any of the numbers.
When tossing a coin there is an EQUAL chance of getting heads or tails.

Tip 2
If you are not marking a probability on a scale you must present it as a **fraction, decimal** or **percentage**.

KEY FACTS

⭐ Number and Algebra

Multiplying Decimals by 10, 100 and 1000
- Shuffle numbers to the left.
- Shuffle numbers to the left once when x 10, twice when x 100 and three times when x 1000.

Dividing Decimals by 10, 100 and 1000
- Shuffle numbers to the right.
- Shuffle numbers to the right once when ÷ by 10, twice when ÷ by 100, and three times when ÷ by 1000.

Negative Numbers
- Integers are just whole numbers.
- When counting from negative up to positive or positive down to negative **remember to count 0!**
- When counting on a number line, count to the right when adding, count to the left when subtracting.

Decimals to two places
- When rounding remember 5 is up! 6.785 = 6.79

Reducing a Fraction to its Simplest Form
- If you are asked to find a **proportion** or **ratio** of two things or numbers you are being asked to find a **fraction** (in its lowest form).

Calculating a Fraction or Percentage
- Remember as many percentage/fraction equivalents as you can:
  $50\% = \frac{1}{2}$ $25\% = \frac{1}{4}$ $75\% = \frac{3}{4}$

  $33\% = $ nearly $\frac{1}{3}$ $66\% = $ nearly $\frac{2}{3}$

Multiplication and Division (with decimal points)
- x and ÷ are opposites.
- Always estimate first. It will help you to get the decimal point in the right place if one is needed.

Checking Your Answers
- Inverse means opposite!
- Check addition by subtraction – and vice versa.
- Check division by multiplication – and vice versa.
- Use 'friendly numbers' when estimating: 2, 5, 10 etc.

Simple Formulae
- **Talk** through the formula in your head. It will make it easier.

Brackets
- Always do brackets in equations first.

Coordinates
- Always read ALONG (x axis) and then UP (y axis).
- Always write (x) before (y) – (x, y).
- Quadrants work **anti-clockwise**.

3 o'clock to 12 o'clock	= Quadrant 1
12 o'clock to 9 o'clock	= Quadrant 2
9 o'clock to 6 o'clock	= Quadrant 3
6 o'clock to 3 o'clock	= Quadrant 4

Shape, Space and Measures

Angles
- Acute Angle = 0–89°
- Right Angle = 90°
- Obtuse Angle = 91–179°
- Straight Line = 180°
- Reflex Angle = 181–359°
- Angles around a POINT always add up to 360° (a complete turn)
- The angles of a TRIANGLE always add up to 180°.

Symmetries
- When drawing reflections remember to keep the correct distance from the mirror line.

Metric and Imperial Conversions (approximate)
- 1 litre = 2.1 pints
- 1 kilogram = 2.2 lbs (pounds)
- 1 mile = 1.6 km
- 1 foot = 30 cm
- 1 pound = 0.454 kg
- 1 inch = 2.5 cm

Estimating Measures
- Milli = very small
- Centi = small
- Kilo = big

Area of a Rectangle
- Area of a Rectangle = length (l) x width (w)
- Area is always unit square (cm^2, m^2, mm^2)

Handling Data

Mean, Median, Range, Mode
- Mean = sum of all numbers divided by number of numbers
- Median = middle number in sequence (always write down in order first)
- Range = difference between highest and lowest number
- Mode = most common value

Charts and Graphs
- Be careful and accurate. Use a sharp pencil.
- Pie charts are good for %, fractions or decimals.

Probability Scale
- Always goes from 0 to 1 (you need fractions/decimals here)

0	0.25	0.5	0.75	1
Impossible	Less likely	Even chance	More likely	Certain

Tips and Technique

Before the test

1 When you revise, try revising a 'little and often' rather than in long sessions.

2 Learn your multiplication facts up to 10 x 10 so that you can recall them instantly. These are your tools for performing your calculations.

3 Revise with a friend. You can encourage and learn from each other.

4 Get a good night's sleep the night before.

5 Make sure you have breakfast!

6 Be prepared – bring your own pens and pencils and wear a watch to check the time as you go.

During the test

1 Don't rush the first few questions. These tend to be quite straightforward, so don't make any silly mistakes.

2 As you know by now, READ THE QUESTION THEN READ IT AGAIN.

3 If you get stuck, don't linger on the same question – move on! You can come back to it later.

4 Never leave a multiple choice question. Guess if you really can't work out the answer.

5 Check to see how many marks a question is worth. Have you 'earned' those marks with your answer?

6 Check your answers after each question. You can use the inverse method or the rounding method. Does your answer look correct?

7 Be aware of the time. After 20 minutes, check to see how far you have got.

8   Try to leave a couple of minutes at the end to read through what you have written.

9   Always show your working out. You may get a mark for showing you have gone through the correct procedure even if your answer is wrong.

10 Don't leave any questions unanswered. In the two minutes you have left yourself at the end, make an educated guess at the questions you really couldn't do.

11 Remember, as long as you have done your best, nobody can ask for more. Only you will know if that is the case. Good luck!

Things to remember

1   Don't panic! If you see a difficult question, take your time, re-read it and have a go!

2   Check every question and every page to be sure you don't miss any! Some questions will want two answers.

3   If a question is about measuring, always write in the UNIT of MEASUREMENT (e.g. cm, l, kg).

4   Don't be afraid to ask a teacher for anything you need, such as tracing paper or a protractor.

5   Write neatly – if you want to change an answer, put a line through it and write beside the answer box.

6   Always double-check your answers.

The 2003 SATs

Key Facts

✦   The Key Stage 2 National Tests (or SATs) take place in the middle of May in Year 6. You will be tested on Maths, English and Science.

✦   The tests take place in your school and will be marked by examiners – not your teacher!

✦   You will get your results in July, two months after you take the tests.

✦   Most children will get a Level 4 or above with about 30% getting to Level 5 (though this varies in each subject).

✦   Individual test scores are not made public but a school's combined scores are published in what are commonly known as league tables.

The Maths National Tests

You will take three tests in Maths:

Mental Maths Test – This test will be played to you on a cassette. You will have to answer the questions mentally within 5, 10 or 15 seconds. This test will take about 20 minutes.

Test A – The non-calculator test. This test requires quick answers on a test paper. You will not be able to use a calculator but should show any working you do.

Test B – This test allows you to use a calculator and includes problems that will take you longer to solve.

STOP PRESS

Using and Applying Mathematics – There will be more questions testing how you use and apply your mathematical knowledge in different situations. This includes knowing what is the important information in the questions, how to check your results, describing things mathematically using common symbols and diagrams, and explaining your reasons for conclusions that you make.

Much of the book is written to help you get into practice for these questions (especially when we ask you to 'read the question then read it again'! It is also worth looking at these pages, which should help you with this area of Maths: pages 14–15, pages 54–55 and pages 58–59

Answers

Level 4 Tricky Bits

Page 7 – Calculators Practice Questions
1) 1308   2) 99.9   3) 80.25   4) 582.9

Page 10 – The 24 Hour Clock
1) 5hrs and 52 mins   2) 11hrs and 27 minutes   3) 6hrs and 46 minutes

Level 5

Page 14 – Checking Your Answers
1) 3312   2) 1320   3) 594   4) 7485

Page 15 – Checking Your Answers
1) 6248   2) 4212   3) 289   4) 46

Page 17 – Multiplying and Dividing by 10, 100 and 1000
1) 370   2) 100   3) 3   4) 0.46   5) 10   6) 6.5

Page 19 – Decimals
1) 41.67   2) £6.14

Page 20 – Reducing a Fraction to its Simplest Form
1) $\frac{1}{3}$ 2) $\frac{3}{8}$ 3) $\frac{3}{4}$ 4) $\frac{4}{7}$

Page 21 – Reducing a Fraction to its Simplest Form
1) $\frac{1}{3}$ 2) $\frac{1}{4}$

Page 23 – Calculating Fractions or Percentages
1) 375 cm   2) 64 kg   3) £91   4) 520 ml
1) 32%   2) 35%   3) 13%

Page 25 – Multiplication and Division
1) 18   2) 71   3) 31
4) 12 635   5) 65 736   6) 12

Page 27 – Negative Numbers
1) -7°, -5°, -2°, 0°, 3°   2) –43, –35, –21, 6, 17   3) -23°   4) 15°

Page 29 – Simple Formulae
1) T = £9   2) N = 5   3) P = £18
Formula A = 5J + 4

Page 31 – Brackets
1) 10 842   2) 884   3) 10   4) 11

Page 34 – Coordinates
1) (-3, -2) = 3rd Quadrant
    (-2, 1) = 2nd Quadrant
    (1, 3) = 1st Quadrant
2) (1, 0) (2, -2) (5, -2) (4, 0)

Page 39 – Angles
1) (a) 15°   (b) 50°   (c) 72°
2) (a) 288°   (b) 250°   (c) 332°
3) (a) 90° – right angle   (b) 135° (approx) – obtuse angle
    (c) 225° (approx) – reflex angle   (d) 45° (approx) – acute angle
4)

5) 55°

Page 42 – Symmetries of 2D Shapes
1) (a)   (b)   (c)   (d)

2) (a) ✗   (b) ✓   (c) ✗   (d) ✓

Page 43 – Symmetries of 2D Shapes
3) (a) ✓   (b) ✗   (c) ✓

Page 44 – Metric Equivalents of Imperial Units
1) 2.27 kg   2) 15 pints

Page 45 – Metric Equivalents of Imperial Units
1) 2500 grams   2) 2.66 litres

Page 47 – Estimating with Measures
1) (a) – (d) These will vary in estimates and actual measures dependent on your book, table, classroom and playgro
2) (a) kilograms (b) kilometres   (c) litres   (d) grams   (e) millimetres
    (f) centilitres (g) tonnes   (h) metres   (i) millilitres

Page 49 – Finding the area of a rectangle
1) 1580 cm²   2) 49 m²

Page 50 – Finding the Mean
1) 6   2) 24

Page 51 – Finding the Median
21 years

Page 52 – Finding the Range
Range of visitors = 47 879 visitors

Page 53 – Finding the Mode
Modal mark = 6.5

Page 55 – Interpreting Graphs and Pie Charts
(a) 3400 yen
(b) 4900 yen
(c) £3.50
(d) £6.75

Page 57 – Probabilities
1) (a) $\frac{1}{3}$ or 0.33 or 33%